Lilacs in Lavender Light

Lilacs in Lavender Light

Don Gutteridge

First Edition

Hidden Brook Press
www.HiddenBrookPress.com
writers@HiddenBrookPress.com

Copyright © 2020 Hidden Brook Press
Copyright © 2020 Don Gutteridge

All rights for poems revert to the author. All rights for book, layout and design remain with Hidden Brook Press. No part of this book may be reproduced except by a reviewer who may quote brief passages in a review. The use of any part of this publication reproduced, transmitted in any form or by any means, electronic, mechanical, photocopied, recorded or otherwise stored in a retrieval system without prior written consent of the publisher is an infringement of the copyright law.

Lilacs in Lavender Light
by Don Gutteridge

Cover Design – Sol Terlson Kennedy
Layout and Design – Richard M. Grove

Typeset in Garamond
Printed and bound in USA
Distributed in USA by Ingram,
    in Canada by Hidden Brook Distribution

Library and Archives Canada Cataloguing in Publication

Title: Lilacs in lavender light / Don Gutteridge.
Names: Gutteridge, Don, 1937- author.
Description: Poems.
Identifiers: Canadiana 20200286862 | ISBN 9781989786062 (softcover)
Classification: LCC PS8513.U85 L53 2020 | DDC C811/.54—dc23

To Richard (Tai) Grove,
in appreciation of your loyal support.

Table of Contents

- Inside – *p. 3*
- Romance – *p. 4*
- Time's Tick – *p. 5*
- Oval – *p. 6*
- Chum – *p. 7*
- Legacy – *p. 8*
- Rude Awakening – *p. 9*
- New Bones – *p. 10*
- Bonding – *p. 11*
- Luck – *p. 12*
- Storyteller – *p. 13*
- That's How It's Done – *p. 14*
- Music of the Muses – *p. 15*
- Tillage – *p. 16*
- Inked – *p. 17*
- Long-Ago – *p. 18*
- Going for the Grail – *p. 19*
- Saw – *p. 20*
- Wish – *p. 21*
- Vise – *p. 22*
- As I Walked Out – *p. 23*
- Waddle – *p. 24*

   SEVEN FOR ANNE in loving memory

- Gift Outright – *p. 25*
- The Seasons as They Come – *p. 26*
- Lament – *p. 27*
- Truce – *p. 28*
- Adieu – *p. 29*
- Genesis – *p. 30*

– Perchance – *p. 31*
– Cry – *p. 32*
– Rhapsody – *p. 33*
– Penchant – *p. 34*
– Gifts – *p. 35*
– Aura – *p. 36*
– Full-Bodied – *p. 37*
– Ironic – *p. 38*
– Contemplation – *p. 39*
– No Words – *p. 40*
– Tenderness – *p. 41*
– Anywhere Else – *p. 42*
– Just – *p. 43*
– Grin – *p. 44*
– Gentle – *p. 45*
– Winter – *p. 46*
– Boredom – *p. 47*
– Moot – *p. 48*
– Regret – *p. 49*
– Summer in the Time of Plague – *p. 50*
– Praise – *p. 51*
– Breech – *p. 52*
– Pluck – *p. 53*
– Gait – p. 54
– Vet – *p. 55*
– Bloodless – *p. 56*
– Moniker – *p. 57*
– Bright – *p. 58*
– Linked – *p. 59*
– Amber – *p. 60*
– Exulting – *p. 61*

– Touch – *p. 62*
– Gibbous – *p. 63*
– Greening – p. 64
– Throb – *p. 65*
– In the Bone – *p. 66*
– Radium – *p. 67*
– Alight – *p. 68*
– Bouquet – *p. 69*
– Elapse – *p. 70*
– Tropes – *p. 71*
– Spin – *p. 72*
– Green and Growing – *p. 73*
– Itch – *p. 74*
– Ghosts – *p. 75*
– Gleam – *p. 76*
– When the Dream Ends – *p. 77*
– Cruise – *p. 78*
– Ritual – *p. 79*
– Gardens – *p. 80*
– Perseverance – *p. 81*
– Distance – *p. 82*
– Companions – *p. 83*
– The Silence Between the Stars – *p. 84*
– Soft and Low – *p. 85*
– Bard – p. 86
– Serene – *p. 87*
– When the Dream Ends – *p. 88*
– Bolt – *p. 89*

About the Author – *p. 91*

lilacs in Lavender Light

Inside

Curly-haired Shirley
doing the can-can
on grandfather's lawn,
strutting her stuff and flinging
her lovely long legs
so high wide and handsome
we burst into prolonged applause
and Shirley grins her little-
girl grin as if
to say, "Seen enough?"
that leaves us singing inside.

Romance

They said it was just puppy
love, but what right
did "they" have to tell
the world what romance is?
After all, when we strolled
hand-in-glove or called
each other "dear"
or traded soulful glances,
I didn't know down from up
or if the moon still whirled
in its oracular orbit, but nothing
really mattered except
the feeling we shared: of sheer
unjaded delight.

Time's Tick

On a sun-strummed September
morning we abandon our summer
cocoons and hit the high
road for school, passing
Leckie's farm where Holsteins
graze lazily and shorthorns
remember themselves
and on past Gunn's place
where hogs wallow like hippos
with snouts in the snuffling mud
and the pasture where Grace grips
her stallion with incising thighs
and the hawthorn hedge where this
year's colt burgeons
his brand-new erection
(and the girls blush lushly
and the boys sing inside)
and in the haze ahead
sits the brick-coat
box we will inhabit
until the sprouting of Spring
releases us and I shout
for the sheer joy of titillating
Time's tick.

Oval

Under the amber oval
of Mara's lamp and all
along Monck Street,
lavished by moonlight,
we play our ritual game,
and Nancy and I contrive
to share a shimmer of shadow
and for a lucid moment
we do a duo's dance
and I, no Lancelot,
espy a careless thigh
and harbour thoughts of ravishment.

Chum

When Marilyn, my chum from school,
in the first bloom of her girl-
hood (with curls as wisped
as winter wheat), sauntered
past the hired hand
and me, the latter thumbed
his crotch, grinned and said,
"Now ain't that a sweet piece!"
and I wondered what part
of her he meant and what
made it sweet.

Legacy

The widow Bray stands
there alone, bee-
deep in her tenderly-groomed
garden (with poppies bleeding
scarlet, roses as red
as a bride's blush and violets
as lush as lavender), watches
the drones, pulsing with pollen,
do their dizzying dance
to apprise the hive of her blossoms'
whereabouts, and thrives
in her flowered bower like a
bloom-inducing wizard
despite the legacy of her loss.

Rude Awakening

And once again we're gathered
in Hendrie's crude coop,
boys and girls lusting
after something other
than the skin they were born to,
showing off our male
merchandise and hoping
for just one peek
at whatever the girls were squeezing
between their thighs and we were
all cock-a-hoop
and as nude as Eve when the leaf
fell away from the pout
of her pudendum and the world
was in for a rude awakening.

New Bones

When my chum Shirley
grew into her new bones,
the boys on the beach ogled
the rogue swerves and curves
curtailed by her one-piece
suit (too shy
to try their luck, too
boggled to breathe), but I alone
felt my heart hum
like a muted flute when she smiled
at me with a will, as if
to say, "The summer's come
and we are here, two friends
still."

Bonding

My father and I go hunting,
twelve gauges slung
over our arms, ambling
side by side, kicking
at every brush-pile
and bramble bush as the afternoon
wears softly on in hopes
that some prey would startle
and there was no need
for the warmth of words until
a cottontail leaps out
and zigzags away;
"Fire!" and I do, wincing
at the rough recoil, but the rabbit
keeps running and Dad says,
"It's only a rabbit," and I say,
"I'm glad I missed."

Luck

As luck would have it, Bonny
and Sharon agreed to play
"Show me yours" and Bonny
lifted her skirts thigh-
high to expose the puckered
pink rose that lay there
winking up at us,
and when I revealed my stubby
stalk, Sharon said, "Donny,
what do we do now?"
and none of us knew what or how.

Storyteller

For Bob in loving memory

You were my first audience
as we lay side by side
in the comfortable dark, and I
spun my bedtime
dramas about meddlesome rabbits
and bumptious bears, and when
I added voices to my creations,
you murmured, "Ah, that's Bingo,'
or "Oh yes, that must be Peewee,"
and laugh in all the right
places and forgive me my flaws,
and I am so grateful
you made a storyteller out of me
and more so now you are gone
and I still speak into the welcoming
dark and listen for your applause

That's How It's Done

My Dad and I fishing
on Mitchell's Bay, and I watch
in awe at the lazy, lofted
loop of his plug and its soft
plop on the weed-rich
shallow and when a pike
as big as a barnacled barracuda
strikes, he sets the hook
with an infinitesimal tug
and waits for the finned wriggler
to break the surface, its muscling
arc bent like Robin's bow,
defying the grasp of gravity,
but the fight is over, the game
won, and my father grins
at me as if to say,
'That's how it's done!"
and I wish the day would last
forever.

Music of the Muses

I was born with a village in my genes
and the spillage of its sunshine
settled in my soul, and I walked out
each memorable morning
word-perfect and poaching
poems by any means,
the mettle of my mind simmering
with simile and tropes about Cobalt-
blue waters and meadows
suborned by milkweed
and dunes seething with silkened
sand and lilacs breathing
lavender light onto
grandfather's lawn as green
as the glens of Eden, and I grew
anew into each iambic
day, tuned to the music
of the Muses.

Tillage

Each Spring morning
I walk into the wakening world
with the sun haloed on the horizon
above First Bush
and strewing the streets and every
coign and corner with bedizening
light and I wend my way
across the milkweed
meadow below the Bridge
where tender-tipped shoots
upburst from their root
and I stroll along the blue-
hued Lake and its self-
renewing waves and on
past dunes as ancient
as Adam's entry into Eden
and I feel the heave of all
things living and spend
my day purloining poems
from the rich tillage of my home
ground and letting them sing
to my soul.

Inked

Under Mara's lamp
and a night-sky as black
as a jackdaw's paw,
blinking stars and lit
by a molten moon, we play
the games our forebears
played when their world was young
and innocence was inked in their genes,
and, boys and girls together
and jolted by joy, they have no
need to heed the disembodied
gods of the cosmos.

Long-Ago
With a nod to Michael Ondaatje

I remember the long-ago days
of my youth, when every morning
was a rebirth and we were like
butterflies fluttering free
from their wombed cocoons
in the lucid air over
grandfather's lilac hedge
blooming voluminous and we had
no brink but the blue
embrace of Lake and River
and First Bush where the celibate
sun rose righteous
and I ambled iambic, past
Mara's lamp on is pilgrim
pole, prefacing poems
as I went, to the water's edge,
where I dipped my pen in Ink
Lake and wrote myself whole.

Going for the Grail

Under the amber oval
of Mara's lamp we gathered
for hide-and-go-seek
and in the marinade of moonlight
shadows shiver and loom
and I find myself huddled
with Nancy beneath Foster's
handy verandah and the rub
of a random thigh is like
a bruise in my blood and I want
to love like Lancelot going
for the Grail with thunder in his genes
while the Earth cruises in its universe
and we all abide.

Saw

When Shirley spins the bottle,
I will it to point my way,
praying for the pleasure of a
chaste kiss, but when
our bodies almost meet,
something akin to raw,
unthrottled desire seizes me
sweet and I think of God's
odd look and that old saw:
sin in haste, repent
at leisure.

Wish

My Dad and I fishing
on Mitchell's Bay, and I watch
in awe at the lazy, lofted
loop of his plug and its soft
plop on the weed-rich
shallow and when a pike
as big as a barnacled barracuda
strikes, he sets the hook
with an infinitesimal tug
and waits for the finned wriggler
to break the surface, its muscling
arc bent like Robin's bow,
defying the grasp of gravity,
but the fight is over, the game
won, and my father grins
at me as if to say,
'That's how it's done!"
and I wish the day would last
forever.

Vise

Next door to Hendrie's
abandoned coop, a bantam
rooster with his quickening cockade
is harassing his harem, and the girls
decide to play Truth
or Dare and Jo-Anne, forgoing
Truth, announces "The proof
is in the pudding!" and drops
her pants, whetting our wicks,
and we can't take our eyes
off that velvet vise.

As I Walked Out

As I walked out upon
the town that loosed me from the womb
and June enthused the morning
with serenities of sunshine
strumming the streets, and the green
Eden of grandfather's lawn
greeted me outright
and I meandered the village
verges like an Argonaut savouring
the sea and soon found myself
in the milkweed meadow
where tiger-tinted Monarchs
fluttered their two-mooned
wings and nectar-noshing
bees hummed a Polonaisean
tune and I came at last
and always to Canatara
with wavelets lipping the shore-
line intimate and the dunes
stood there as wind-stroked
as the day God uttered,
"Let There Be Light!"
and I opened my iambicized eyes
and the Muses spoke.

Waddle

My Dad on skates: as silken
as a swan mirroring a pond,
and me, just eight,
on my maiden blades, gliding
on my ankles in a desperate effort
to bond with a man I hadn't seen
for five years and more
than one war between us, and I tried
not to notice the surprise
in his eyes, the disbelief
that any son of his could waddle
like a duck on ice and handle
a hockey stick like a dazed
bassoon, and I was grateful
to the gods, whatever their ilk,
who let me wobble beyond
his wounded gaze.

SEVEN FOR ANNE in loving memory

Gift Outright
With a nod to Robert Frost

We couldn't afford a photographer,
so here we are on brother-
in-law's lawn in the only
black-and-white recording
of a moment beyond the nuptials:
the two of us on tip-toe,
leaning into the dream in the
other's eyes, your chin
up-tilted to capture my kiss
as I embrace the joyous geography
of your face, and I want to promise you
fifty-seven seasons
of uninterrupted love
my gift outright.

The Seasons as They Come

Now that you are gone
summer skies are not
so blue, the demise of autumn's
leaves is more subdued,
winter's snow sifts
less softly and the bulb-burst
of spring brings no
relief from my bereavement pain,
and so it is I face
the seasons as they come, hold
aloft our having loved,
acknowledge the gift of your grace
and carry on.

Lament

I wake and feel the luff
of the dark and when I reach
for you, you are gone and I am
alone in a bed big
enough for two, and our love
like a star fixed in the firmament
or a candle with twin wicks
still burns anew,
and I try not to feel forsaken

Truce

We find ourselves on the Bruce
Trail, weaving our way
through sprays of spruce and cedars
and over denuded hummocks
where limestone protrudes
like nicotined teeth, and after
a while we hold hands
as lovers do when touch
is triumphant, and let summer's
celibate sun simmer
through the screen of trees
and brush us with such tenderness
I want to hug you from here
to Heaven and feel the rush
of our moon-lucid love,
knowing that our lives are always
and ever making a truce
with the gods.

Adieu

In the midst of my grieving
I forgive you your leaving,
for ours was a love rooted
in passion that mellowed with the years
like a June moon and we grew
in unison like the rings of a slow
oak and I am comforted
at the last by the memories that linger
and loll and by the stalwart
sting of my tears as I bid you
adieu.

Genesis

For fifty-seven years
we fashioned our lives in the same
furrow, tilted the odds
in our favour, and I loved you
with a poet's passion, you who
came to me like the gracious gift
of a benevolent God, who redeemed
all things under Heaven,
you who were the doyen of my dreams
and the genesis of my joy.

Perchance

In this dream I stand
alone on Canatara, listening
to the slow inwashing of waves
and wishing you were no longer
unalive and we could share
our summers once more,
feeling the sun's beneficent
beam thrive on our upturned
faces (and speaking in code
like a bee-dance in a hive)
or blinking in the light from the arch
of stars above us or never
again having to query
the perchance of our brave love
or its whereabouts.

Cry

Mrs. Bradley could be heard
in the far verges of the village,
setting tongues a-buzz,
and Gran and I watched her
solitary on her front porch,
uttering a bone-chilling
cry in search of some
word that would tell her
where she was.

Rhapsody

My village re-imagines itself
each morning when the sun
rises over First Bush
where robins rhapsodize
and the streets and alleys, etched
in the muscle of my memory, throb
with mist-mellowed light
and I greet them like Adam
dreaming in Eden's perpetual
day and I wend my way
iambic to Canatara's rapturous
sands where on-shore
breezes blow like the breath
of a loose-limbed bellows
and rustle the silken curls
of the sea-grasses and I want
 to capture such passing home-
grown mementoes in the rhymed
crucible of a poem.

Penchant

As a teen I was less than dashing,
had no pimple-face bravado,
and when she smiled at me
on Rondeau beach, I gave her
a lop-sided grin,
in return, and I must confess
to surprise when we found ourselves
coupled in the back seat
of a Ford Mustang, where,
with little adieu, she essayed
a French kiss, our tongues
torqueing lustily in a fullthrottled
embrace and for the
first time I thought:
even girls have a penchant
for passion.

Gifts
For Tom

You and I jigging
for walleye wriggling
for prey in the weed-rich
underwater meadows
of Cameron's Baltic blue,
(and hoping later on
for a smallmouth or two)
and seated side by side
and savouring the sun on the gunwales,
we lay our rods down
and let the afternoon drift
by under a day-
time moon marooned
in the southern sky, and the happiness
we feel, the exultation
of these moments are truly
gifs from the gods.

Aura

My first love poem
was an ode to Laura Haggith
whom I worshipped from afar until
the day she rode shotgun
in my father's thirty-nine
Dodge and I drove up
and down the main drag,
showing her off like a prize
rose or the aura of a new-
born star, her youthful
beauty unblemished
by my futile ogle or the rogue
feelings I fought to hide
or the hodge-podge of my hammering
heart.

Full-Bodied

When Virginal Eve sampled
the apple from the Tree of Knowledge,
she knew her nakedness
and festooned it with a fig-leaf
and Adam felt the first
of several moon-induced
urges and everywhere
in the ruined garden tulips
bloomed before dying
and lilacs on the hedges withered
before budding again
and all things grew autumnal
after the seeds' seethe
and the un-Edened pair
soon found themselves
dithered and digging
but still cheering the god
who'd made them the perfect
example of the human hunger
for love and a full-bodied
world.

Ironic

It must have seemed ironic
that Abelard's feeling for Héloise
was deemed Platonic when every
letter of every word
of their chaste correspondence
dripped with the lust they were denied
and the abdication of vows
they swore in haste, but love
is love and has been since Eden
when Adam, apple-dazzled,
gave in to the fiery combustion
of desire.

Contemplation
For my mother in loving memory

You tell me you found your mother
cold to the touch, the morning
sun pouring golden
upon the shimmered sheets,
and you but a girl of thirteen,
contemplating death and all
it means and not knowing
of course that I would discover
my own mother without breath,
feigning sleep, and I longed
to feel you warm once
more, your eyes smitten
with a smile, but we are all
hostage to love and loss, to laughter
at our a-borning and weeping at our demise

No Words
For Tom

I remember the first soft
ululation from your crib
two rooms away
and how you danced into each
day and the absolute un-
bibbed joy aloft
in your eyes, O child of my age
who even now, many
years on, can tug
at my tenderness and I wish
you welcome in the world
with these leavening words
though no poem can grace
the page to picture you perfect
and my heart bursts with the love
it can barely contain and I long
once more to hug
you to Heaven.

Tenderness

Who would've thought that such
a summer's afternoon on Cameron's
sun-strummed, pellucid
blue, would find us, fishing
rods in hand, poaching
perch finning soundlessly
a fathom below among the reed-
breathing underwater
glades or if luck holds
a behemoth bass cruising
like a teeth-seizing barracuda,
and I'd rather be here than
anywhere else but Heaven,
touched by tenderness and loving
the plot of our never-ending
story.

Anywhere Else
For Tom

You and I trying our luck
once again on Cameron's
blue flume on a summer's
afternoon, strummed by sun
and a bashful breeze, and we ease
into the rhythm of your rowing
before the anchor is weighed
a full fathom below
where the big-bodied bass
furrow the underwater glades,
probing for perch lurching
to pluck at minnows shivering by,
and above us sits a quicksilver
moon and we are hugged
whole by birch and fir
ten thousand years
in the making, and I'd rather be
here with you and love's
hug than anywhere else
on God's globe.

Just
For Sandy

I was just seventeen
when I caught you in my amorous
eye and fell in love
with your unbudding beauty,
the sudden glamour of your glance
and the way you forgave
my befuddled forays into romance,
and we spent a celibate summer
proving something other
than lust grows gracefully
this side of Heaven.

Grin

For Alvin Gehl

As a non-swimmer I was warned
off the River, but you,
like Huck Finn on the swift
Mississippi, built
yourself a raft and tried
your luck on the mud-loving
Thames, while I stood
ashore like a landlubber,
wanting so much
to be your budding Tom
Sawyer, but you, like any
friend, waved goodbye
with a grin that said, "This
joy is yours."

Gentle
For Tom

Gentle is the word I'd choose
to describe your principled probing
of my oeuvre in this room
where we confer over books
or remark on how a poem
grows like the rings of a slow
oak or how a character
springs to mind fully clothed
and in between weighty
discussions of plot or incidental
ironies I recount the foibles
of a near-forgotten uncle
or ornamental aunt,
and so it is the animating
annals of family and forebears
take reliable root and are passed
on through the genes of the generations
and I will rest with ease,
knowing my work will come
alive again every time
you open a book bearing
our name.

Winter

At grandfather's funeral
I sit and listen to Gran
sobbing quietly, and I feel
my grief deepening, knowing
I will have to live out
my life without the man
whose love was unstinting,
with no ease for my bereavement
pain, and something
like a season has died within,
leaving me to winter alone.

Boredom

Celibate and bored, Eve
dallied among daisies
and daffodils along the groomed
boulevards of Eden, waiting
for a bloom to droop or a bee
to be baffled by honey
or a bullfrog to croon
a Siren song, but nothing
in Paradise grew or seethed
with seed or met a timely
demise, and when an apple
hung succulent on the forbidden
tree, the mother of us all,
unexempt from temptation,
gave it a chew.

Moot

When the great poetaster
fashioned Eden for Adam's
pleasure and, in his haste,
forgot to add passion
to the greenery, so that
when Eve was breathed out of a
spare rib, the mated pair
smiled a lot and admired
the scenery until Eve,
celibate and bored, famished
the forbidden fruit and made
the fate of humankind
moot.

Regret

There wasn't a breath of breeze
in Eden, but then Adam
was no sailor and Eve
no Aphritite,
and it wasn't the sea that un-
did them but rather an appetite
for apples and the ethics of Good
and Evil, and as the ruptured
couple bid adieu
to their paradisal dale,
they paused to think upon
God's oddities and grapple
with the rictus of regret.

Summer in the Time of Plague

I remember well the summer
the pristine beaches of Canatara
were closed, the "No Swimming"
sign propped up in the sand
like a bandaged thumb, and mothers
kept their children handy
in the keep of their kitchen, and we tried
not to notice the friend with a
withered arm or the awkward
angle of a leg-brace,
and nobody knew where or when
"it" would come again
with invisible vibrancy, and we were
afraid to utter that benumbing
phrase: "Infantile paralysis."

Praise

The flowers in the Widow Bray's
groomed garden grew
like a soothsayer's predictions:
poppies, gladioli, daisies
in profusions of bloom, licked
biddable by light and nursed
by a tendrill'd touch, and we prayed
that she found some solace
in the praise of a grateful village.

Breech

You welcomed the world feet-
first, as if to say,
"Here I am, I'm me!"
and when I spotted your perfect
brow, unbruised by the lurch
of birth and your eyes greeting
the room blue, my heart
burst like a rapturous rhyme
with a love that would last us
a lifetime.

Pluck

One lucky day
when June was still jejune,
we gathered in Hendrie's coop
where JoAnne dropped her drawers
without a thought or a blink
to expose the ripe rose
between her thighs,
and the boys, too wise
for their years, on the cusp of lust,
vied to see who was brave enough
to pluck it.

Gait

We never tired of watching
Shirley and her long-legged
gait over grandfather's
lawn or her drum majorette's
prancing dance with fretted
boots and twirling baton
or the twinkle in her eye, just
for me, that implied, "Here
I am, take the bait!"

Vet
For Tom

Even now I see you
moving from farm to farm
and, "doing no harm,"
treating the beasts of the field,
and God's creatures are healed
under your touch as soothing
as the fluting music of Orpheus,
and I remember how
you always loved animals,
how you hugged our malamute
or giggled at a Scottie's impish
antics or calmed our fretting
cat, and you were ever
tugged by love, destined
to metamorphose from boy
to practicing vet.

Bloodless

Every Saturday afternoon
whatever the season, found us
seated at the aging Imperial,
taking in the double-feature
where the silver screen bristled
with Indians and two-gun
paladins in their sagebrush
sagas, where cutout villains
died bloodlessly for our
amusement and the colour cartoon
catapulted Bugs and Magoo
into our midst before the
cliff-hanging serial
teased and tantalized, and O
how we cheered in renewed
communion when the cavalry arrived
in the nick of time and the disparate
parts of our wondrous world
rhymed.

Moniker

For my brother Bob in memoriam

My favourite uncle Christened you
"Googie" from a character in the
funny papers, and "Googie"
you were to all and sundry
in a village numinous with names,
nicknames and monikers
of every ilk, but when you left
the village you left "Googie"
behind, along with the tooth
fairy, Santa and the boogieman,
and after a while it didn't seem
odd to be calling you "Bob."

Bright

What I remember is the lake
of grandfather's lawn,
lilacs in lavender light,
twinned tress brushed
by a big-bellied breeze,
spiraea foaming at the
generous edges, and Gran's
verandah where Jello cooled
in the shade: these are the images
my boyhood teethed on,
embering still through the long
arc of my age and breathing
memories as bright as a
poem on a page.

Linked
For Tom

And once again we find
ourselves on Cameron's lake,
our fishing gear baited
and ready, and an afternoon
slides by as soft as silk
and as rare as a blue moon,
and we dream of the deep dells
below where the big bass
glide, unblinking,
and minnows shiver in the shallows,
and we are comfortable in our own
skin, happy to be here
in one another's company,
sated by sun, linked
by love.

Amber

Tom and I jigging
for pickerel on Cameron's blue
glaze, letting the boat
drift north to south
on the breath of the breeze,
and we ease ourselves into the
amber afternoon until
a big-mouth bass
strikes with a barracuda bite
and we watch it lift with a
whip-lashing whoosh
out of its element like a bent
bow, sashay on its tail,
spit the bait and leave
two fishermen bouche-bé

Exulting

That summer the air
was salty with sex in Hendrie's
henhouse where we exchanged
sly surprises when Jo-Anne
bard her bum and dared
the boys to show "theirs,"
and there was nothing hum-
drum about the petulant
petal envised by her thighs
or the stalwart stalks we brandished
to the world, aroused and exulting.

Touch

For Anne in loving memory

We lie in the lee of the dark
and let moonlight flow
molten over us, and thigh
to thigh we tingle with touch,
and I want so much to hold you
till doomsday dawns,
to watch your bedizening eyes
open to me like a slow-
blooming rose, to canonize you
whole and feel you singing
in my soul.

Gibbous

It must have been a gibbous
moon that night in Nuremburg
so many years ago
(and too soon gone)
when we lay abed gazing
at the stir of stars tingling
in the unmarred dark
above the breeze-brushed
sill, and we were pleased
just to greet one another
eye to wedded eye
and let ourselves be liberated
by love.

Greening

Mrs. Bray's garden was like
that first flowering in Eden
before Eve and the apple,
and though widowed by war,
she moves through the gladioli
and gardenias of her petalled bower
with a Grecian grace, and every
bud she touches bursts
with bloom while the gods
in their greening, smile

Throb

Cockrobins hob-
nobbing at ease on grandfather's
lawn, dreaming of dew-
worms bloated in the grass,
a song of the season throbbing
in their throat.

In the Bone

For Anne in loving memory

I wake from a dream of you
and know you are no longer
with me in the irredeemable
dark of the room we once
loved in, and I feel the moon
looming and the shudder of shadow
across the counterpane,
and I try to bring your face
once again into view,
smiling for me alone,
and I yearn for the soothing bruise
of your embrace to ease the brittle
breaking of my heart and the un-
renounceable ache
buried in the bone.

Radium
For Tom

You and I slow-
rowing over Cameron,
our oars dimpling the surface,
and we are hugged by ante-
diluvian forests of spruce
and pine and birch
(with bark as alabaster as a
nun's wimple), and we
are rinsed by the sun's radium,
silence in the blue above
and silence in the precincts below
(where perch peregrinate and minnows
Wrinkle) and we are happy
to find such un-
encumbered joy in simple
things and pass our days
content with our lot, tugged
by love.

Alight

For Anne in loving memory

I wake and find you alive
and loving beside me,
your eyes alight in the gloom,
and when I realize I'm still
in the desmesne of dream (knowing
that the gods play us like pawns),
I want to hold you there,
safe and abiding, until
Doomsday dawns.

Bouquet

For Anne in loving memory

That first Christmas,
when our love was nicely new,
I sent you a dozen yellow
roses as a sort of mute
tribute, and it seemed
from that moment on
our passion grew, suffice it
to say, like the slow opening
of those roses, and when
I think of you now
beyond the reach of flowered
affection, I would trade more
than one lifetime
for a chance to close
the gap between us
with the perfumed spray of a
rose bouquet.

Elapse

Marybelle Cooper,
my best friend's cousin,
stood behind the white
picket fence that hugged
our yard in her Tartan sweater
under which her just—
about breasts breathed
serenely, and when she smiled
my way, all the sonnets
I longed to sing lapsed
on my lips and when she smiled
again, something tugged me
aside and I knew for the first
time what love was.

Tropes

I was told the first word
I uttered was "No!", as if
I were warning the world of my arrival
and wouldn't take "no"
for an answer, a one-word
poem in hopes of establishing
my bona fides, and soon
I got the knack of nouns,
the vim of verbs and the rigour
of rhyme, and these were the tropes
a poet could drown in.

Spin

Whenever we played "spin
the bottle," I willed it to point
at Shirley and, throttling
my lust, I gave the girl
a chaste kiss, upon
which she grinned and said,
"What a waste!"

Green and Growing

If it's Spring in the Point,
the lilacs on grandfather's
hedge are livid with light
and there is bulb-burst
and fledgling fusion and juiced
buds anointed in the sun's
nuzzle, and I find myself
meandering the milkweed meadow
with a thirst for everything green
and growing, and the air aloft
is soft with the singing of larks
and the drone of home-going
bees, and I have such a
longing to pull the perfect
poem out of blood and bone.

Itch

O it's hard not to be
immortal, for when we are gone,
we live on in the memories
of those who loved us alive
and in the stories they tell
of us when day draws down
and we become part of the lore
that thrives wherever there are
humans with an itch for history,
and so it is, I look upon
my demise with no regard
for endings, compromise
or polite applause, certain
that, against the odds,
the long sentence, my life,
will not be periodic.

Ghosts

Everywhere I look in the
noonday dazzle or under
the slow moon of a summer
evening, I see the ghosts
of those who touched and left
their tender trace: my grand-
father who lived for three
years in the trenches and then
lived again and Gran
aglow in the smiles of the littl'uns
tugging her apron and Uncle
Potsy who loved me until
I grew to love him and my Dad
who skated as smooth as a swan
polishing a pond, whom
I forgave the itch of his addiction
and a host of others: boy-
hood chums and village
vassals who peopled my life
and imperfect poems, who let me
hug the world home.

Gleam

When Jo-Anne dropped her panties
and exposed the prize between
her thighs, she had a gleam
in her eye like Delilah's snipping
Samson's lofty locks,
like Salome's doing her death-
dance unfrocked,
like Bathsheba's dithering David,
or like Eve's outwitting Adam
with an ample apple, and what
I want to know is did they
enjoy the triumph of their titillation?

When the Dream Ends

For Anne in loving memory

I wake and feel the bend
of your body, but when the dream
ends, I am alone in the
condoning dark and you
are still unalive,
but I thank the all-seeing
gods for the tender years
our love thrived and grew
like the incoming rush
of combers on a star-lit
lake and, like larks in the amber
air, we sang the same
home-grown song
and travelled true to the spirit
that bound us beautiful,
and even in death you are
the breath of my being.

Cruise

For Anne in loving memory

You ladled out love as if
there was no end to the gift
of its giving and swathed in the dusting
of moonlight upon
the nuptial bed, you cradled
my lust and made it something
soothing and ceremonial,
and we sent our epithalamium
up to the high Heavens
all the days of our fifty-
seven-year conjugal
cruise.

Ritual

For Anne in loving memory

O how you loved a funeral!
tethered to the T.V.
while Jackie wept in black
and Loretta and Bobby grieved,
their dreams sundered by assassins;
you loved the monumental music,
the oomph of the organ, the silk
of ceremony, feelings fuelled
by eulogy, or lamentations
of lives lost; you watched
it all, pomp and circumstance,
breathless, moved to tears,
awed by the raw ritual
of death's dance.

Gardens

In the milkweed meadow
a stone's throw from grand-
father's yard in the sizzle
of summer, butterflies flutter
at ease on the afternoon breeze,
bees, peregrinating
from flower to flower, nosh
on nectar and, high above,
a lark soars with song,
and I am welcomed into
this paradisal place
as one of the Elect, and I pull
open a plump pod
with its silken secret like Jesus
breaking bread before
the Apostles, and I say a prayer
to the god who fashioned such
gardens for our innocent use.

Perseverance
For Bob Clark

We watch, awe-struck,
as you break your maiden on Hickory
Ridge, taking sixteen
stiff-whiffing practice
strokes and then, back
bent like a fresh pretzel,
you send the ball looping
leftward over a ploughed
field like a dying duck,
and in the certainty that history
does not repeat itself,
you fix your eye upon
a far horizon, pluck up
your pluck and begin again.

Distance

For Anne in loving memory

I wake and feel for your presence
beside me, but I am alone
in the nuptial bed, and I try
to recall the blessings of your body,
your breath upon my brow,
your tendrill'd, tremoring touch,
but these whims even now
are vanishing like moonlight
in the morning mist, like the waning
whispers of a dream, and I
confess that our love, so long
in the making and steadier than a
heartbeat is on the ebb-tide,
for Death has too much
distance, its rupture complete.

Companions
For Colm O'Sullivan in Memoriam

You and I were golfing
companions in our halcyon days
when the sun shone down
upon us and our fairways
as bright as an Irish smile,
and I loved to watch you amble
ahead, rotund and risible,
with a twinkle in your Kerryman's eye
and a gambler's urge to drive
your innocent orb into the
next county and make
your irons sing while lofting
the ball greenward, where,
with a nod to the golfing gods
you sink a ten-footer
and the gallery, charmed by your Gaelic
guile, applauds.

The Silence Between the Stars

In the gloaming over the River
flats (where we sometimes
flew our kites in the big-
breathed wind from the lake),
we played squat-tag
or May I? while the moon
loomed above our random
roaming and threw its mottled
light our way, while we waited
for the sky to darken and ignite
the silence between the stars.

Soft and Low
For Anne in loving memory

Alone at night I sense
your presence in every room
and when I am down, I simply
recall the silken swerve
of your smile or your voice,
like Cordelia's, ever soft
and low or the way you brushed
a curl from your brow or held
horizons in your eyes, and these
small remembrances, these
sweet shudders of delight
touch my heart's core
while your love blooms in my bones
like a sun-rubbed rose.

Bard

I find it hard to imagine
a life without the wizardry
of words: the nuances of nouns
and verbs surging: pinned
in the prism of a poem, where rhyme
has its reasons and rhythm is what
the heart hears in the silence
between beats and simile
has its seasons, and I was born
to pain and poetry, and longed
to embrace the arcane business
of being a bard.

Serene

Serene in Eden, Adam
soon grew tired
of bluebelles and a dozen
cousins forever in full
bloom, and he longed just
once to pluck a blossom
and watch it shrivel, to feel
something akin
to desire, to be uncivil
to the God who sired him
and rubbed Eve like a genii
out of a random rib to nibble
an apple and leave them both
ungrammared.

Embarcation
For Anne in loving memory

I wake in the condoning dark,
desperate for your touch beside me
once again, with moon-
light breaking over the sill,
and once again I summon up
the will to live another
day without you, to find
such solace as I can
in the ache of your absence, wishing
that I could seize on the mysteries
you are now privy to,
that we could come together
in a synchronicity of souls
and embark for the stars.

Bolt

They say that lightning never
strikes the same tree
twice, but in the summer
when I was almost me,
both of the maples that hugged
grandfather's house
and shaded my boyhood
games were struck down
by a single savage bolt,
and the home where I was lavished
by love and jolted with joy
and which I spun into a
dozen pulsing poems
and ringing rhymes, stood
there shivering in the sunshine
like a prude nude, and I knew
then that nothing is ever
the same again.

About the Author

Don Gutteridge was born in Sarnia and raised in the nearby village of Point Edward. He taught High School English for seven years, later becoming a Professor in the Faculty of Education at Western University, where he is now Professor Emeritus. He has published seventy-one books: poetry, fiction and scholarly works in literary criticism and pedagogical theory and practice. He has published twenty-two novels, including the twelve-volume Marc Edwards mystery series, and thirty-eight books of poetry, one of which, Coppermine, was short-listed for the 1973 Governor-General's Award. In 1970 he won the UWO President's Medal for the best periodical poem of that year, "Death at Quebec." Don lives in London, Ontario.

To listen to interviews with the author, go to: http://thereandthen.podbean.com.

www.ingramcontent.com/pod-product-compliance
Lightning Source LLC
Chambersburg PA
CBHW020543080526
44583CB00013B/976